AF379078

Autobiomythography
&
Gallery

poems

Joe Pan

Brooklyn Arts Press · New York

Autobiomythography & Gallery
© 2007 Joe Pan

ISBN-13: 9780978825706

Design by Joe Pan.

Published in the United States of America by:
Brooklyn Arts Press
154 N 9th St #1
Brooklyn, NY 11249
WWW.BROOKLYNARTSPRESS.COM
info@BrooklynArtsPress.com

Library of Congress Control Number
2006907615

FOURTH PRINTING, APRIL 2015

This book is dedicated to Dawn, Chris, Johnny, & Wendy.

I also wish to thank my family & friends, & the readers who made suggestions over the years it took to put this book together: Stuart Dischell, Claudia Keelan, Bob Hass, Jim Galvin, Reed Smith, Rachel Beck, Chris Cook, Tim Krchmarik, Dean Young, Marvin Bell, Elizabeth Fels, Jim Clark, Tim Liu, Spencer Short, Fred Chappell, Christine Garren, Cheeni Rao, & Wendy Pan—I owe a debt to each of you. I wish to thank those responsible for the various small awards & prizes that helped with time & rent, the Iowa Writers' Workshop for the solitude, space, & medication, the women of the Center for Conferences & Amy Margolis of the Iowa Summer Writing Festival for the employment & laughter, as well as the editors of those journals who first gave homes to some of these poems, including: *Boston Review, Denver Quarterly, Greensboro Review, Mudlark,* et al. I'd also like to thank the Cubs for keeping me joyfully distracted during the more difficult months, when the writing of these poems occurred.

Contents

Autobiomythography

WHAT IS GIVEN

All things being equal, I'd say the world
was most interested in its own piracy,
engaged in constant erasure. The February snow
a kind of performance art involving light
and weight dispersal, the wind hastening behind
like paparazzi in a celestial cover-up. The earth
immured, retracting. A neighborhood dog kennels
its muzzle in a dead tire, scavenging for warmth.
If death is natural, as we believe, then the death
of the world is natural. Nature's mistake was creating
its own weaknesses, and all things are made in the likeness
of that divorce. The red truck sliding through a stoplight
near Governor Ave is a form of subtraction, the twin bars
of an equals sign narrated by tire tracks. It jumps the curb,
careening headlong through a chickenwire fence.
When the driver gets out, he is shaken. He cannot
articulate. This narrative should have ended in death.
The world retracts. Between conscious moments lies
these moments of stilled belief, of inquisitive imminence.
There in the snow the driver looks awkward, looks
skyward, looks down. He discovers only himself,
but that is a given.

Autobiomythography

Library of Congress Cataloging-in-Publication Data
b. 1979
The stories of BD'JP.
Contents: Royce—Hollow—A Room Forever—[etc.]
1. West Virginia—Fiction.   I. Title.
2. IA, NY—Wishful Invention of Life & Praise
PS0102.A100 2001 2007'.1 56-7681276

Silently he gouged the double-bark of pine
until it bled. Corralled by limestone ridge and hollers
the August weather seeped into the valley floor,
mercurial, the slate mist cupped and emptied from a palm,
suspending the glass song of a hermit thrush among
the canopies. Uncle Royce wiped the blade along his jeans
as the elder pine giggled out its sap. *"You seen
a blue tick matted with this stuff? Best glue Nature
ever gave, pitch."* I was convinced we'd gathered there
for sport, to spy on sassy jailbait plucking fungus
from the wet earth, later skinny-dipping up at
Shawnee Creek. Wed myself to thoughts of near-conception.
"Fun's plenty. But ass don't pay the gas." Later, skunk-drunk,
Royce climbed into a neighbor's cage to spar a bear
chained to a stump, and lost. Pine glue held closed his casket.

Flat shoes fit on like gaskets—Uncle Royce in dreams.
Lilac, soot, corrosive agents. Words could
not describe the loss, his smells; what makes
a man? Identity's a lozenge on the tongue
and once dissolved leaves but red words;want
not;man reduced to math/myth/moniker.
I worked the mines until the bank foreclosed
our home and level went the logging acres.
I prayed for chokedamp, swampgas, whatnot—come
what may. Come chariot of fire, come long drunk,
come factory and chemical, river
water blushed with nitrates, runoff from pig
farms further upstream. Gone Fishin. Gone Fuckin.
I couldn't hold my alcohol or any job
and all was left you couldn't shake a stick at.

Stuck it out a short while in a motor home splash indigo.
Rehashed a rubbished religion. Reduxed. Detoxed
in a truck stop shower stall: en route, one-way trip.
Left home to let my anchor float freely. Desired clemency:
a star released from orbiters. Dear God and whatnot,
Dear Royce. Spit-shined moon what waned above this helpless
ne'er-do-well, reflective. I hitched from a trucker name of
Harvey, let me knock off in his cab. Soon my thoughts of West
Virginia fell off a cliff and leapt at verdure foothills
where aphids circled crepe myrtle, snapped to apogee.
Heat glassing up the asphalt, whistling till my mouth
turned silt. He asked where I was headed, said
he would quit near Halifax, VA. The hills
were all I knew, I said. "Well bud," he said, "You best
learn something new real quick." I slept the death of colliers.

I longed for coal dusk, concrete street signs, jailbirds coiled
by newspaper stands, jaybirds hugging the dark phonewires.
I'd capped my upsets/insults in a bottle and chucked it
to the curb. Sunrise over Greensboro, NC—   mopped up
and rung through thunderheads. THE BIG PICTURE gone blank.
Pumped gas for board. Barwoman's belly
cause for breathlessness, grandeur of fleshy thighs
I clutched like death in my motel room; romped
on Frigidaire and foldout—plumb rocked her body
into cradle   but the womb unbuckled.
Here's the heart performing Hide and Seek,
the heart memorial, like some airy portico
and ancient bust split through by invisible
weather. 2x2 we boarded the ark, and for what great hope?
Two souls arced—snuffed out like a rocket.

Twin aches like rocket boosters=Royce, Unborn.
You wake and have to rise because it's what you do.
My honey's note pinned to the lamp like a fresh outlook.
Blinds drawn, bath drawn. Bubbles like a thousand tongues
of regret. She asked me to forget her name so I tattooed it
to a kumquat rind and skipped it 'cross the reservoir.
Days past, drew breath, upchucked. I went rowdy,
raucous. Wore my special hat. Lost a four eights draw
to four kings, and nearly killed. Were there a trophy
for self-deprecation, I'd have offered up my pose.
"Robber bees are born that way," said Television.
That's a mouthful, I replied, and quit my new construction job
for an art less on the level. I worked at making
every home seem emptier while I was there—I stole.
Deprived of all but profits. Depraved and sucking bottles.

Derivation of *Fiasco*—a bottle.
Corked—but screwed, at sea. No note.
Or one that no one wants to read at least.
I found the definition in this book
on the Italian language for beginners.
First Edition, stolen as I stole the rest
to sell online to bibliophiles/colporteur
dealers accessing the legalized
Black Market. Lady at the library desk
got me computer savvy; what duffered less
in cyberspace I bartered at the pawns.
Fiasco—night. The luminous waters batwinged
upside a houseboat docked near lakeside villas,
my hands full with stereo equipment: then
someone flipped a switch to start the motor.

I flip out. My brain: rack and pinion/piston:
misfires. Pretty soon I'm drifting at lake's center,
listening as the motor cuts, still unwilling
to move an inch. I stay that way an hour, till dawn
polishes a door frame, slants between the shutters.
On some Great Chain of Tension, gravity upscales muscles
and the stereo loses its life for it. The wind
cries through a porthole. Time unhinges and drifts like so
many gulls and still nobody comes to check
the noise. It's cold. I want whatever is going to happen
to happen, so I rub my arms and walk upstairs.
The fibroid dawn, pinks and yelloworanges, smeared
in the *reality of dream*. On deck a black man
in blue jeans glares hard from beneath a baseball cap.
A gun balloons one hand like a fiddler crab's.

Befuddled—gone and worn my guardian angel out.
The shore was too long away on deepish water,
so I propped an elbow on the rail and spit.
Him: "What's your name son? Where you from exactly?"
I give you that, I give it all away.
Him: "Way I see it, you got two choices. None good.
What was that I heard you bust inside?"
A stereo, but it was junk. Old hi-fi.
Him: "There's nothing inside that's junk. You notice
everything's baroque?" *It looked okay to me.*
Him: "Not broke, you idiot. Fancy. Paid for."
He laughed and I was sure he'd kill me.
I'll do what it takes to make things right. Whatever.
Him: "I know you will. The Sheriff'll see to that."
Hey now, let's talk. How's 'bout I pay you back in books?

I wasn't booked. I spilled my guts, hoping for
some leniency. Mister R. P. Warren Whittier
was proud, middle-aged, and kind. A writer, he understood
the mind's not strong enough to kill a heart for good, nor
hold it long before it starts to struggle with the cage.
"Everyone can find a problem," he said. "But few
can find solutions." Pawned my near everything for cash,
him waiting in my truck. When we returned he offered
me a job as he pocketed what all I owed and owned,
including books, which he filed in his library.
I did groundswork/gruntwork: supersaturated
particles in his solution. Slept in a spare room
and read most often. No TV. We fished, swapped
whopper stories of our famous aches and loves;
our nightly walks a kind of peripatetic poetry.

He got me penning nightly my elemental haunts—
brainturf, loinache, deathdrive—drop my guard,
put it all on paper. Said life was less for my
ignoring it. Made me search out over the land,
asked what I saw. *Pretty stuff, some.* He said "Man is
wolf to man, son, and all alike." Said, "Parcel out
the newly missing from the freshly lost. Repopulate, Deucalion."
I read his books and craved my own, my land and place,
my voice. Set out again in quietude: charted the past
from recall: Coffindaffer crosses crowning hilltops,
frying ramps with molly moochers, coal dust, plantlife,
the glass factory, rivers and union church. Soon Royce.
Royce arrived with nightmares, brought the Unborn.
Wrote that. Wore that. Swore and wept that. Won that rebirth.
And buried myself in our tragedies and hopes, mining life.

Self Portrait, as in Divisible

Passing a book on Feng Shui in the mirrored hallway
I instead open another on the paintings of Botero
where the purity of deformed spheres seems
to both mock and praise reality's
obesity, while attempting to stir
an argument on the multiplicities
of life: that we are only alike as
the likeness of some original.
                          Ocelot, my cat,
is a woolsucker. His large yellow-chipped green eyes
slandering, splintering, muscles contracting orgasmically
as he grips the riverrock-colored afghan
and draws out the empty milk of a memory, and is fed by it.
He has learned this from no one.
He folds up and sleeps in the opulence of brain.
Is he an occurrence of form
or its ghost? Seeming both the pattern
and the thing itself, he is even more
than that, being also an idea, which survives
within me, snatched however briefly from extinction.
This is how we are changed and made new.
We are the idea of ourselves driven into being.
Our bodies fit to form as we create the patterns.
All mirrors are wrong. There is no such thing as imitation.

Zero Effect

It seems that everything is moving
away from me, boxy compacts
driving beyond the last fenceposts,
pool balls dropping into pockets.
A kind of theft, really, how the small dog
inhales my breath as I reach down
to pet it before it scampers away.
Even my most insidious poker face
has seen my well-earned dollars
drift southward in the arms of friends harvesting
their shiny cranberries from the money bog.
Wanna go another round? Hell, hit me.
Vector formulas and stratagem of battle,
pickup lines and names for faces, stout
and slippery as language. There is nothing
so silent as soup mopped up with wheat bread,
a cat eclipsing pages from a book, and there I go,
outgrowing the sweat and skin of me,
fidgeting to loosen each ribbon of nuance.
There was a time once when I would never
have said there was a time once.
See that nothing flowering
between each star? So what about it.
There's me pondering the twenty-seven
corners of my apartment from the tub, twenty
minutes behind schedule, that person I could be
clipping and straightening a necktie,
a bagel in his mouth. I go after him
but the floor is wet. Perpetually wet.
The flakes of dead skin remain innumerable.
There's this hat I flip cards in, black and oval,
lined with silk, inscribed with a name
in black magic marker. I try on the hat. I try
on the name and it fits.

Animus Mundi

Johnny was determined to be the last man
to walk on the moon. He thought to wear
a big boot, read from a speech he devised
on the toilet. Johnny said once that lice
were reincarnated diamonds. He could dance
the Charleston but only before the Venetian
gesso mirror in his bedroom. Johnny played fairly,
voted out of sincere faith in decency and justice.
At twelve, he read to his invisible friend Justice
from the Song of Solomon and woke to rapid firings
under his bedsheets. He would ingest
four-leaf clovers for even better luck.
Johnny ate fried rice with pork rinds
and doused every dish with steak sauce.
If you knew Johnny you would
understand. One day he read his own
obituary and played scratched Twenties
records for two days before he called
the newspaper to report his survival.
They were not pleased. That night he curled up
by his bed, naked in his Special Forces
uniform. After rain he stamped the female moon
from puddles. Johnny felt the ghosts at his back.
Long sleek accusations rattled in his ear,
so he showered with the door open.
The ghosts were everywhere he looked:
the eye of a red dog, the curve of coffee
spoons, tips of waterproof matches.
Johnny felt uncomfortable around cathode-
ray tubes and chrome. He once test-drove

"

a wooden lizard at a theme park. The words *Free
Generation* made him dizzy enough to hiccup bile,
he said. He recognized the smell of Bengal tigers.
Johnny knew how to snap the vertebrae
with a rope he used as a belt. Sometimes
he slept outdoors, in the mud, in the rain,
the air conditioner chopping wind like a helicopter.
He kept a condom under the receiver in his phone.
Johnny felt he sounded sexy on the phone,
a new tremor in his voice. Johnny drank gin
with plastic ice-cubes and memorized the license
plate of each car that passed his apartment
that first summer he returned. When the physician
uttered his condition he nodded and drove
home and looked it up in Webster's College
and laughed. Origami butterflies died
strange deaths in his hands. He thought
if he were handsome, he could marshal
a parade as batons twirled asterisks
overhead, brighter than fragmentation
grenades. Johnny was in the market
for a good pair of scissors. He would
cut out the eyes from magazine models
and paste them on the bathroom door.
Johnny loved the sun more than anything,
though believing himself to be allergic to it.
Johnny admired how his muscles twitched
when he flexed his knuckles around a roll
of quarters. His body was an unwieldy tool.
He believed he had never set foot in a tattoo
parlor before, that the smeared green images
rose from a small, compact location
in his center: chakra and chi and navel.
Johnny had a running joke with himself:
he would be the first person to spaceship a monkey
into the sun. Whenever he thought about it
the tears just kept coming.

The Smithsonian Guide to North American Shapes

Rhombus, the

Notorious lush, half-brother to the diamond,
it leans to touch what upright forms will have it.
The engine/transmission mounting points of our fathers'
Oldsmobiles (1949-63) had trained this shape to sturdiness.
The perfect cube, tilted, displays in three dimensions
its one expression. On a six-sided prism it was, perhaps,
the window Newton watched Truth course color through.
Its sides imply risk with no eventual point of contact
save its beginnings. It continues beyond the perspective of pictures.
The parallels angle to fit a genus of conch shell,
and true to its worth, despite Goebbels terming all irregulars
Judeonegroid, as if it were a slander, the rhombus—
one crooner's slang for "abstract ideal of Jazz"— avails
to some physicians as form of female genitalia during birth,
and thus, the shape of humans.

Gin

The linkages (bare-wired) gone watt & red hot,
sun-stamped earth, wait for me seamstress
of the double hemisphere, ruby-clawed hopeful bird.
Berry-ginner of the lower Guadalupe, when in flight
you danced my twin dreams of you: cross-current dandelion
freed of concentration / unbidden wind-driven dart.
Wick-feathered funky dropped-down smoothed-over
thing, light chasing from your movement, announcing
your arrival in broad colors. The stars reconciled & remitted:
there should have been no world not blue for you, warmed
about a dew-dipped belly, caramel & yellow dappled
Pekinese of the Pouty Lip, but beakwise—the whole
stage gone sour beneath: the proliferation of garbage piles,
the railway intercoastal and toxic sludge puddles. If I
found the right words (redressed?) I could keep you
safe in language, syllable bound & yes, language a trap
in itself, validation through intonation, not much braver
than silence, but hopeful. Man's unmatched missions of mutability
unwound your wristwatch, warbler, leaving you fobbed
& forgotten. It's hard to convince the living the value of
the near-dead not dying when death confirms their living;
no chain of being but a coat which fits us all just once.
The linkages burn & burn—a white needle thinning
through thinning fabric like a javelin unraveling air.
The world's great coat tightens like a lozenge in the throat.

The Hog Men

These are the last days of the hog men.
Their balled fists strangle what is not there.
An apronned figure among the snow-bit woods
scratches an armpit of dried soap
and sings through the zero of her heart.

The woods are on fire behind her.
The woods are bleating.
The woods are clapping around her.
The hogs roll their eyes in the stockyard,
ramming their snouts between pen bars,
baring their tongues to the dirt.

There are fewer shotgun shells than hogs
and fewer hog men.
Some will never work this job again
knowing what they know now—this paradox of savior.
What was meant for the slaughter must have freedom.
The released bear their teeth to the new dusk
and race for the light.

What they are left with,
and what they will always be left with is this:
The bounty of ash, of cloven foot,
this sweet-smelling corona of hog eye.

The Contaminant

The sound was abominable. It cleared the air
of rain and settled on a square patch of rosaries.
The eucalyptus could not stand the green gods
gave it; the sound was probably never heard.

It woke me with a shatter. From the dream I woke
with a spine of eucalyptus hickies stitched to my stomach
& coffee in the air, a woman missing, a steady silence broken
steadily by the kitchen faucet's faux-menstruation.

The day at first proved normal. No impish puns, no miracles
that seemed inopportune or appropriately destined.
Churches open, meat market closed. Barbs of fascinated
children poked one by one from behind the church fence

as I passed, delighted by a patch of cloud-light
splayed across a brick wall. The crowds passed by
about their business, tattered business jackets, oiled eyes,
their ties somewhere between a spring and winter.

A silk beetle shivered in my breast pocket, which I
mistook for love, and tweezered it out with my fingers,
holding it aloft. It had no spoken name. Instead it hummed.
Love me, it hummed. Louder. I squashed it like a god.

Past Judgment

In the new world, everything is ice
and factories. Clutter is a rule rather
than a way of life. Some miss the smell
of juniper crushed in the palm. Wires
congress overhead and what isn't loss?

In the small world things condensed
re-friction, fabricate the possible.
There are no senses but a sensitivity to
other small things. They make the new world.
They rub against each other in sex and prayer.

Tiny blubbery blue-eyed pink fledgling
bird in my palm ebbing breaths, chirpless
strategy for life, frenzied with ants
like a transient disease, you are between
two worlds and complicate these matters.

I might leave you to frizzle (fragile
neck of melted rubberbands,
möbius intestinal track translucent
in the spring sun under dogwood),
I might frock you in my pocket.

But the small world things are myopic
and fashionably resistant to the problem of death.
All they know is congregation and
displacement. Let us be like them.
In Cocoa Village there's a small, clean

bookstore near the mint-green ocean
known for undertow. It has good coffee.

Slight Fit

All clouds are the new
retro.

Each mystifies
the next, an apparition
of apparatus.

Here comes the next big
thing—a camel squeezed through
a needle squeezed through the engines
of a private jet.

Reality is just Time slipping
on a skin. War is a lonely
hot date with itself.

Sit back. Here's the part
we imagine ourselves.

Livid

O Cinctured Somebody, my mirror-light-cusped somnambulist, all
I ever wanted was to clasp your palatable data to my hard drive—why
bow to shower water before the Patron Saint of the Profane, old knock-knee-
hearted me? Well, my pithy lapse in tithing the People their bottomless
cups of Want unburdened my billfold. O brothers! My former partner's
gone AWOL in Iowa, but not my Left Hand Man, my lovely
pewter-colored computer (screen-saved by decollated digitronic
lapdog), handsomely ornate, a virtual biography of *beck* and *call*,
fly-eyed, with one roosted in a private chatroom linked via cable
via camera to your shower stall, O showering next-door Somebody.
My pixilated pixie, your split-ends splayed by a roof-cistern's draining
runoff of ruddy rainwater in one of the faux-French deals I had installed
before my labor worker layoffs. Water is not a passing through but a coming
into thing, awash in light & spectral like you, minor matinee idol,
reduxable instant celebrity for the livid cybermoonlighters grown dim
with LIVE! downloadable id. The unexamined life is not worth living
or leaving unexamined.

The Second Fall   (a character study)

Funes the Memorious categorized the leaves
Of a sapling, branded each with a new name, those
Set with the quicklime of time, ever industrious
& hungry for moment, for minutiae. For what?
A horror. The mind cannot let go. Come noon
In Babylon I walked the frail flames with Shadrach,
Meshach & Abed-nego under the golden
Idol of Nebuchadnezzar, breaching the subjects
Of stifling economies, mule specimens &
The momentary weakness of significance
Before all is made trivial by some momentary insight.
Each were assured in our assurances: we'd be saved.
It was good to chat beyond celestial obligation.
Sub-Conscious, hid in instant, I suddenly sensed God could not
See or hear me (Aye, Caliban upon Setebos—'Will sprawl,
Not that the heat of day is best, / Flat on his belly
In the pit's much mire) & so I bestowed upon the boys
A vision I would pass to others: Lizard—belly-slumped
on a sanguine beach—miraculously transformed into a man
In an iridescent flash of evolution.
I shrug at their big questions. It is not for anyone
To know. All is package & record. History
Is a salted slug, the shriveling of conclusions,
Guesstimations, protocol.

***

He hands me a trumpet as I mount Pestilence.
There are too many eyes upon me now to turn and flee.
& what if He should hear me, sneak up on me
& steal the plumèd spine that straightens me, kneeling, along this cross
                                        of judicial servitude?
Perhaps these thoughts are best left drowned in quietude.

***

Post-SecondComing, post-HowGreatThouArt, wrestling
On the white granite peak of Mt. Harney, South Dakota
With Honest Jon of the Lakota & a biker named Larry Unsung

Motored in for the Sturgis Rally. We breath hard & deep like old Victrolas
Into the deepening valleys; wondering now if I did right in sparing, now sparring,
Able men under this illegitimate sun—I smash their groins like gourds amid
                                        the cottonwood & ponderosa.

***

Mountains crumbled to crumbcake & I chose not to fight the fallen in Christ
& sudden clang & whoosh of Me, felled by my brothers' blood butter-brown swords
& left behind. We fought as if no love had passed between us,
                                O cloudless centuries

Moment of self-awareness as felled guardian, Gideon, eon-fluxed
Man who wouldn't bow to Baal & then angelic henchman & again my human
Form fits me like Pascal's coat, hemmed with the possible apology.

Every one of you a One, a sudden stranger wrought with history
None heard the first crack in the firmament (nor the last)
Being too attuned to one time, one place—and so blind to the Great War

Understand that I endure you: compost heaps & banner ads & motor vehicle tren
It bothered him that the dog at three fourteen (as seen from the side)
Should have the same name as the dog at three fifteen (seen from the front)

Panoramopticondemic. Awash in scene, witnessed by the Viewer omnipresent,
Alienated from the affection of that voice which shards like lightning.
Two Mormon boys buy me soup & I listen & worsen & wissen

Q: If the beast is trained to kill, where goes that blood-memory
     once beast is conditioned to live anticlimactically among the domestics?
A: It prowls the archetypes. It broods over its own milky bones. It lies in wait

Gott weiss ich will   Not of the philosophers
Kein   Not of the intellectuals
Engel sein   Not of not of

                I, out of the order of angels, can hear you. What strikes you
        as beauty is nothing
                                but the beginning of terror

***

Death arrives in two ways: a) Quickly b) Not so quickly. The bull, blood soaking its spindly hide, knelt before the stands. There is no better life than mine, no longer among the monasteries. It is a true world that turns its back on its people. He still enjoyed playing tetherball with a Coke can tied with fishing line to a birch. A flashlight ambering a solid fifth of Kentucky straight bourbon. Withering harpsichord, you amplify my freshest feelings of regret. The beach crystallized by night's spangled armada. The glib orchestral ring suddenly adopts a stance of unforgiving lightning. Living is often confused with survival. The young girl read aloud from her book: *the opalescent eel churns its electric body music beneath a thick, wet skin.* A horribly pragmatic take on abortion: take it out, put it on a table—does it live? And talk of loadstone and sea granite. *One man's moral aperitif is another man's hard edge of reason.* A talent may often rely on the negation of itself; keep in mind the calculated withdraws of the pugilist. The beauty of the labia unfolding is briefly platonic. It is the pain of categorization to label fingers *digits.* I take notes so that I can forget more often; thought is simply an emptying of the crowded mind to make room for more emptiness; I write to forget. I felt less when I knew more. Compassion happens when someone is tired of someone else not having anywhere to hide. The true gift given to humanity by the cosmos is the ability to ignore; this is why man has power over the gods, yet no true power over his own heart, which cannot be ignored. The gift given to humanity by the heart is its ability to replace the cosmos with other people. This is how we all became beautiful gods unto ourselves. Watch us fall & fall & fall.

Ghost of Gaudí Caught in a Tower of the Sagrada Família

Standard-issued trumpet & cement chaingang of precious fruit
       Heaven & Earth, rivalry unto contempt
       there is nothing in this next world that I could not have had in that
triangle, grape, palm tree

Hosanna   if I could dream it would not be dreams of corn
sacrificed motifs
       symbols on the faces of flipped coins

Let my fear be based in fantasy

A visitor says
Herod stands over the geese & murdered babies

Let the tortoise bear my weight
       watch again as the tram
  passes through me
not metro blocks away

Here there are tabletops with wings
       mopeds in the summer
wind-chill factors

Barcelona. I have no meaning for now

Once in a land and there you have it
As a child in Reus, I kept pace on a donkey
       because of the rheumatism
I've seen the best of both worlds turn
                their backs

Old man drafting a tower where he would wind up as the tower's dream
Motley ornamental privately-funded spectacle of God
Gent de camp, gent de lamp, temper like a red bird slingshot from a hat

Flickering anatomy of a hollow reptile   the shimmer of what is missing
The visitors teach me. Mediterranean Gothicatholic
Calvary at noon & magnanimous Passion
              Otherworld?   I am the unnatural litmus

              I stay because there is nowhere else to go

Raku brimming with blast furnace colors
Green cypress with pigeons piercing its lip

My brother would break the shoes in for me
              blue and gold of desire, my land of honey
the four-barred shield and St. George in the square

The driver thought my body was a vagabond's
pomegranate head with its uncoiled rope of fire

I cannot die, Barcelona. It is not finished

                         Rose window with triumphal brow
                    peering into the ribcage of a stillborn

Memory of the Body (III)
The Micro-Pointillist, Devolved

What was I eating the first time I heard color and fire
were not tangibles   but events?
                                                  what was I wearing?
                                                          hopefully something blistering and vivi
so that I dotted these events about my canvas   tight as riches
and thrust my fine hands through eternal.

A detonation of denotation. The final CLAP! Hush now icicle. Hush now empty frame.
There in the stone garden   the last stone passenger pigeon
a form crazed in two from weather pressure
wet from the first spring rain,   the memory of its first body   (the stoney hilltop)
extinguished   among household plants.
                          My kinsman—all small things grown large return to their reduced forr
On the patio I sit and drink piña coladas   and shots of liquid cocaine   with a bowl
of raspberries, slightly chilled.   The cataclysm of the known world   erupting
over itself   reversed, re-engineered   laying tracks for new hegemony— this can happen
anywhere,   in a backyard such as this,   looking out at children on swings, chained
to some euphoric energy.
                                                  Hush now.

The mind crazed with event.   The self as color and fire.
The detonation brought on by the new   dismantling   the new   dismantling.
New thought   new world.   We all work like this.
Changing your mind means adjustment in consciousness.
That's why I used to love tending garden.   Each new color was a tune-up.

But learning requires an undoing of something else.   'Yes, and now I know better.'
If one believes in betterment. And is not the end of something
the beginning of something else's end   and their collision in time   the event of being?
 and that moment simply
a replacement part from the world's endless storage facility?
                                          larger than the ash&rubbished
(and newly refurbished)
Library of Alexandria.   (& newly ashed).

How each moment I
          detonate suicidally
          with recreation—

Ode from an Apprentice
-after Humphries and Fitzgerald after Horace

You've claimed more little deaths than the Titanic.
Half the boys in town notched up your headboard &
Took your feather pillows in their mouths (a lover's panic)
For what you've smirked & called Communion of the Damned.

But the young men come less often, don't they, Seth.
Midnight raps that once led you downstairs to your proscenium
(In silk kimono, a Bordeaux import on your breath)
Haunt you now on alcoholic nights as woodpeckers
Turn your front porch into beachside condominiums.

If your buckled door had been less easy at the hinges
These nights might not have grown such tongueless hours;
I've comforted your X-lovers, held their hands as dawn mirages
Reddened their eyes, kept them up with chess & Sweet & Sours,

Spoke as gently as a mother, though years their minor; their hopes
Like inchworms in the creases of my palm. I refused whatever cash.
Half those simpletons were all pumped-up on dope
But still it mattered. Watching them sleep, humanity was somehow thicker.
Sometimes they'd cry your name and bring me to a blush.

From your alley apartment, the myrtle melting to a dark mustard,
You watch me pass with my new lovers on our way for beers.
In your old age that leather belt has lost its luster—
Still, you'd stick it in a knothole to relive the glory years.

The Smithsonian Guide to North American Shapes

New Hotel Developed During Recession

Architectural nib—wound lofty, uppity even,
constructed effervescently, saintly skyward blueward against
a bright backdrop—HOTEL—pasted there. A sheen like magic,
like the magical enterprise of music, lit up, steelshine
windows and *glossy-corporate* a color now, a compilation
of lost colors, weightless in the beachsalt air, aloft,
a compendium of antiearth, aboveitall, americhrist.
Maybe I'm just reaching. But there, arisen where dunes
reigned and seaoats perked their views, a tower,
a new thing blinding the sunset, with summer pools a mile's
fraction from the surf, haloed by seagulls, a breach in terrain,
archiving tyrannically whatever rebuffs it: baker's shop
and sandwich tent, pavilion, boardwalk, what ebbs and ebbs
against its borders. My eyeshift pastes it there. Hotel lit
on the cloud mountains, over the sandhills, where surfers keep
their watching, their voices bleared by treble/and bassthumps cars procure/
where hoisted to the heavens/it stunts us at the shore.
Refrain. It's hard to. I grew up sculpting castles near these dunes.
But now, what could obscure that...weightless...watermirage? And
why not wash my hands of it? Because it lacks essence.
It demonstrates without allowances. A building is no ocean.
Peninsular carcinoma, unleash your querulous nest of jetlagged snowbirds.
Bathe the town in burnt red and watery knots of bubbleflesh. Why
not. This isn't paradise. It's funny. How I act surprised, as if you
weren't expected. Truth is, the lawyers saw you coming.
This transient land's watched apostles topple the apostates, subjugate
the everglades, evergreens, canes, groves, cattail river gates in search
of goldpower. Grabit&growl. Get your tickets for the Fountain-of-Youth.
What's changed? The industry of Florida is disparity and space.
Even the wild pigs are not our own.
My words seem lousy failures, but this is what I've got instead of money.
I'd pay a hurricane but you're proofed for it. You'll be empty in a decade,
though you'll already have succeeded in bringing down your winters.

Memory of the Body (II)
The Child, as I Knew Her

Within these confines: two leafless cogs ground out
the dulled red berryseed of a sapling: twenty finger
lanterns: plump eggplant hunched in its black universe.
A throb of hysteria resounds: whale calls transmitted
through Campbell's soup cans soul-strung by feeding wire,
or was it only the vacuum cleaner sputtering
through its necessary ritual beneath the dust cloth?
                                                   And if I say
this child is imagined, that the midnight phonecall
from the X-lover never arrived, would you be surprised
to learn that I have loved that child? that I ran cool oil
over its hips: scoured the odors from its crevices
and read the folds of her eyelids like unearthed scrolls:
the halophyte of the fist: and to break from its unbridled
clench would snap off my good wing?
                                                        I've watched
the votive candles burn through vats of rubber
as my daughter whispered *stars*. I've glided through a wandering
drunk and mouthed her precious curls as she slept,
one arm behind her head like a suicide, and have charged
a god with her current keep at an open casket wake.
                                                          Don't you ever
tell me I haven't got what it takes to love, because
I'm in the mind of nails and warring factions
and the other end of this line is dead.

Brunch with Mrs. Edwards

Mrs. Edwards concurs. There must be life
On other planets. She loves Hawaii. The big
One. There are soaps to be made, bicycles
& sunglasses, statues, lamps & bougainvillea.
She feels someone must hold us all responsible.

Mrs. Edwards knows that when the Dow
Drops, gas & new technology is strictly off limits.
So are new handbags. Conservation goes into effect.
A sensible person simply does not gallivant
Around, flashing $ in "the poor's ravenous eyes."

Mrs. Edwards believes in life after death,
The constant invisible, the white light & tunnel.
She went under the knife, *tuck, tuck, snip*
& woke with a new face to meet the faces
Of the dead, fogging up her mind like a cataract.

Mrs. Edwards has her many vials: blue, velvet,
Cream. Her ups & downs. Her little helpers.
The sunlight is too credible, too steely. It waits
In rearview mirrors, windshields. Rain's ruined
Her knees. Her son sends rare bark from Brazil.

Mrs. Edwards loves her sugar. People deserve
Better, she says. She recycles & reprimands
Columnists in *The Times* for misrepresenting
The aging Boomers. We support the charities!
We banished fur! We saved the whales & Serbs!

Or was it Croats? Mrs. Edwards cannot believe her eyes.
The old neighborhoods have gone to hell with rival gangs
& towers gone. Reminisces on the old Broadway.
Her second husband left, she says, for lack of oral sex.
They kept it open. She missed her men & lunches.

She wants the concierge of loneliness to retire.
To give up & go. Her exotic finches lay their heads
On cold mirrors in the cages, gray breath like liquid
Fire fogging their apparitions. They are unwilling
To chirp the worksong of those born in captivity.

Mrs. Edwards says she has this urge. I will set
Them free tomorrow, she says. Tomorrow I'll
Transit tunnels, the express, the turnpike, to Father's
Dock in Browns Mills overlooking the cranberry
Bogs, and let them go. Or drown them. Or us all.

Mrs. Edwards feels she is out of options.
We sit on the patio, snacking on plantains.
The only pure thing in life, she says, is detestation;
Everything else must be answered for. I light her
Cigarette & smile. The price of sex is conversation.

Ode to Tobacco

Tobacco that lewd effervescence of death
a streamlined hysterical blue wing of smoke
ground cough of the body utopian pleasure
I'll smoke till molasses catch flies in my chimney

plutonium please just hand me a Camel
I'm not even kidding I'll smoke till I croak
these motherless nipples moved Freud to consider
neurotic reactions to internal pressures

so I'm nursing for life

green elephant ears frayed by dusk's choreography
on foothills of North Carolina's topography
permissive as druggists instructing the redwood
on living too well marauder of capital mass importation of wealth
from the Chinese who smoke thirty million fresh packs in an hour

clear cellophane wrapper pure crinkle of promise cocooned like
the Imogen Cunningham photo invisible
women asleep in white blouses
the odor of winter parched woodburning stove
a general's slogan tattooed on its waistline

dried brain of cicada
unequivocally cinema

Newing: a Lifestrut

Failed staff inflates to devil's walking stick.
Fall in Spring, & you walk the talk.
The walking stick & a bit of whiskey
in the gut. Say things like
The sky tonight is rich in ethereal industry.
The creambelt of nimbus, jetstream turfwars.
Gone now the bobbing crab apple
that daily ripens & plummets like a stock.
Forget the diagnosis of osteoporosis
Falstaff—just don't forget your cane.
Sell the percocet and crystal meth to neighbor's kids
& move on down the boardwalk.
A caravan of mermaids pass,
blues & seagreens & naked breasts & old
men gumming coneydogs.
You've changed your life
& now you change your life
again. & now? You've got
a battery of selves, a fuselage
of conquering constructs.
Change again. Do it again.
You must lose your lives
to live one.

The Sicilian Bull

Wild finch, free-thing, you are too quick for this poem!

But bull, broadbacked, tempered brass bull you
are not. Horns hooked like the brass moon, stretched
by the meaty palm of Perillus, the voice you low
is your creator's. You were a king's final word.
But Perillus did not catch the irony
of his name in time. Here he thought his life's
great gift—you bull—was to make a fire chamber
for the kingdom's crooks. Your hatchback beat the Beetle's.
Your belly a place, once heated, broiled the hearts
of humans condemned for being born Medieval poor.
Poor bull, their screams are your true voice,
a slave voice, bellowing from a ballpean-
battered pit. Poor Perillus, the artist's curse,
to be trapped and cooked in your creation.
But Perillus! The lowly bull lowing is how we know you meant it:
device of slow torture, imaginative industry of death.
You got what you deserved, buddy, sliding out its brass asshole.

The Sportsfisherman Responds
to the Fish King with No Wishes

Dream-eyed, antediluvian fish, I canonize you
in the name of the leadweight pellet, hairy
ferret-tufted lure we call the rooster tail,
scaleglint ripplets near the Coralville Dam
in latest September. Flat-headed panfish
of the Near-inedible Bonies, I give you gravity,
which is the tug of death,
raised now in a light your subaqueous truths
ignored. A wisp of chimney smoke lights on the lip
of dusk while I imagine you imagine home a final time.
In the rocky gorges you flashed and scuttled, the hollowed trunk
harbor where your cities sprawl. The cache of your mind a flutter
of dashes. Dangling at this angle, you shiver bitterly like guilt.
It is probably not enough to tell you some evenings I walk
the brickyards lonely along the river home
and watch rings widen on the water
in wavering ellipses until they grow beyond
reconcilement. Lately, the earth giving underfoot
feels sturdier in my catch's absence,
nor is the unburdening of my gear
among the rotting apples not a relief. If anything
I'd wish to be oblivious as God to the tribulations
culled by near-death fishy wishes. The conflict lies
in moralizing pain in plainest pleasures, which
if anything is what the sporting's all about. I must put
you back, though I would guess, with the roles reversed,
you'd serve me up to turkey buzzards. As if the moon
were the flashing bottom of a pail in darkness
and I were the one bottom-slinking sunk and breathless drowsing.
What can I say? Empathy may not be something to be found
at either end of a monofilament line, or along
the redbrick paths of a honest hunger. You eat fish
yourself, no? and wish for more. But this is my choice,
beyond the wishing, and I wish for fish no more.

Labor under Curse: for Jason

Our tragedy today is a general and universal
physical fear so long sustained by now that
we can even bear it. There are no longer
problems of the spirit. There is only one
question: When will I be blown up?
W. F., Nobel Speech

.

The salt-struck air off the strand decompresses over
the green dragon at the confluence of two rivers—
concrete scales green as shelf-life, fledgling dragons
at the coquina base. Anchored to a river island mythic
in the village sense, where sailboats lick its harbor
free of antecedents—waiting for *ever*. The story goes
an angel, masculine & primitive, subcontracted,
bade the dreaming sculptor design a dragon to meet
the Eau Gallie Causeway traffic with charmed
indifference, lest the island sink, which it did,
two inches a day, which is the rate I grew
from Jan 1st-Feb 1st, 1986, measured against
a doorframe, which is where I'd say the contest
between me & the finite world began.

..

Legend also had it that once wombed inside the dragon's belly:
a warhead, pornographic, timed for temperature
to bump from Cold to Hot & so the loss
of Georgia & inevitable retaliation. The apotheosis of dogs & cats,
all lit up and thrust skyward in tableau
among the wafts of boiled swamp cabbage,
snook, blue crab, lightbulbs, love, above the coast
that slipped a disc, spread supine its vertebrae of hotels
& discount malls. Nostalgic weapon? Lest we forgive our debtors.
This is how rain feels on its one-way mission
to puddledom. I imagine my brother Jason, a roofer,
lays down his hammer, looks slantwise & upward,
pines flowering with the lit filigrees of disaster, O Tannenbaum
gone Disneytechnic: virtual—virtueless—vanquishing.

...

The waves like billfolds opening, fluttering, folding.
The layers of phosphorous the moon silk-screened on the shells
of sebaceous loggerhead turtles shimmer like an afterbirth.
We go to the beach to get drunk & whisper in the conch's ear
the sour language of forgiveness, a humble tutelage,
amassing & destroying all the wealth
of a childhood severe in its orchestration,
a violent
pithy
nature.
If you look at a star too long it disappears, so we spent
the night undoing, until the sky went barren with our interest
& the moon logged-off in the southwest
corner between Key West and Tampa Bay.

....

The smell of an orange blossom gives voice to the blossom.
A yellow sort of speech raised to drop its dropsy baritone.
Without loss there is no recovery, no record, no chord plunked.
What is most frightening in life is a possible loss of that recovery.
The ocean building to aria, Sturm & Dranging over the impassible dunes.
The ocean filled our empty ears with chatter, which we refilled
with talk of mole crabs, elliptical remarks, whistles, beach glass &
wandered up the coast like twin weathervanes
drawn to separate distances on the same axis, two wind-worn painted dragons
cut from a tin coffeepot inscribed with: *And the Poor Will Always Be ---- Us*.
We have agreed that I should die before him.
We have agreed that neither of us should ever die.
And suddenly the sky flares up. A thin hot wire illuminating the darkness
                                        over Cape Canaveral.
Satellite on a rocket, launched, now a rogue missile gone astray & detonated &
                        descent   scent
                                    descent.

What I Meant to Say

The sea is half of it, the Other
is the other half.

This after the driftwood bearing our initials drifts past sight.
Before your plane dips a wing
into the overripe sun.

You only knew the half of it.

I'm on the beach with mirrors
signaling you home,
aware that even if you noticed the sporadic flashes
you would not turn back.

An incredulous sandpiper
the size of a fallen halfmoon
gets one good look at itself before
the brass wave overturns its body.

I wish your plane would turn to stone.

The Hurricane

It begins by blowing sandpipers sideways, manacling coco-de-mer palms with metal chains from garbage cans used to keep the raccoons out. It's the first of the last days, rain plowing roads with the opposite of nihilism: the everything, the too much, the irretrievable. The eye has moved beyond us, biblical, causing battery-powered radios to bark on, startling crickets from the sink drain. All eye and no heart and yet charged with an imagination; sucking up small toads from the St Johns River, kiting their aerated husks over the Melbourne Causeway. We watch from inside a café where two yellow strips of masking tape bisect windows at the diagonals. We play chess and feed crumbs to a Husky whose owner confides in us that in a former life he was King Solomon, and had it been his decision to make again, he would have sliced the child in two, 'Since everyone's so skilled at lying.' We venture outdoors. Car alarms protest the hail now golfball size which ping and pank their starred signatures in white. Gales tunnel the avenues, sending up newspaper leafs like planes taking off from a destroyer. The horrifying beds the beautiful. The sublime drenches our pants and presses our spines to the brick wall. The heavens are falling, we think—simultaneously thinking, I imagine, because we share the same body under an umbrella blown outward and I would rather not be two minds in a hurricane than one.

Memory of the Body (IV)
The Indulger of Larger Anatomies of Self

It is possible we have grown emotional
opposable thumbs
                (I can almost sense the weight of this new hammer)
which lack any viable means of expression.

It is possible that we can finally feel each other.

I find myself sometimes believing there are fringes   (ok parenthesis)(ok auras)
outlining the body   which when punctured by acceptance   of *us*
as everything else, leak   our very natural selves
into the external   very natural   Self   so that we can no longer identify ourselve
from et cetera, bungalows, catamarans, shuttlecocks, kumquats, garrets,
Appalachia, marsupials, gingivitis, eyestalks, kakapos, jerky
          {your world here}
which when punctured
hitch our blazing *basics* to the jetstream

                                        one grand unifying
                                        vanishing act.

The problem is   there are neuro-firings that misread the shadows at the hinge,
miscommunicate the fresh blossom scent rising in an empty room,
so that our sense of a shared Internal   which may or may not be false
is at least mistrusted. Can we trust our own responses enough
to believe they can be globalized, when everyday we discount
the simple false epiphanies from the day before?

Perhaps eventually all feelings will be entirely recorded as nonexclusive
from the events in which they take part, rather than sensations
one struggles to define internally and then attempt to share.
"My lover left me. This produces feelings I know you know,
because you are me and I am also the lover that left us."

Which is painfully sad, if you ask me.

Perhaps we will go the other way, attempting to maximize
expression by crowding the feeling with language
until it bursts from the flesh like a splinter:
"At 4:15 and 21 seconds on Friday etc in the auburn dusklight
radiating behind the etc my lover left me
and there is this thing in me that struggles to stay afloat and a place
that feels like bees."

Our sympathy doesn't require the whole of the story—
though sometimes it is difficult   as in religion
and perhaps as dangerous
to take that leap
that 'philosophical suicide' as Camus put it   into belief
into trusting that someone understands you.

Until that time when all is known in shared significance
we manage.
At least there is no stopping the self from desiring to trust itself.
Bodies tend to trust their own histories.
Even pain tells us who we are.

You Know How it Feels
to Inherit Tragedy

—For D.L.

Twin gargoyles resting, legs crossed, wings cushioning their slumps,
beaks like a pair of a pair of pliers.

Before we apply the necessary clamps, try not to think *electricity*.
Try to remember your birth and that first rubbery knot of light.

The farmer moved about his crops, testing the wind with dirt,
knowing one of his sons must die and one must bear the mark.

When the boy who'd run away woke, the eighteen-wheeler
was gone, his bags were gone, he looked down by his sides
along the road's shoulder. He still had no arms. A fog muzzled
the streetlamp down the road. The healer kept his fifty dollars.

The skiff coasts gently into the cavities of night.
Stars loiter like pennies in a well
where hands are pulled from hands, or wash
the grime from knuckles before suppertime.
There came a time her hands forgot their stations
at the side, at the wrists,
above the cobbled street in a vacant room
where dresser drawers left open
offered nothing and the stairs creaked in expectation of my weight
as if all she remembered in the salt air was this.
She'd lost the cradle that grips a child's crayon loose in tight fingers.
She let our child slip into the ocean.
The Coast Guard would not find her
before she drifted into the Gulf of Mexico.

A shadow caws for its black coat then turns and nods.
It spreads its two wings, Music and Urgency.
It pours the bugle noise from its blank heart.
It rains its bellied hatred through the glass parade of buildings,
slantwise rolling its shadow over downtown buses
never challenging the truth behind the sound it makes.

Victorian. The roof's spine struck with termite scoliosis.
He recalls how the bristle he erased from fatmen clung like shadows
flung to each unmounted stool in his barber shop.
A hushed cigar is crumpled by the stone mailbox.
He rips each corner of the envelope and begins to eat.
A woman watches from a basement window.

Halved birds. They sang their bodies through windows, shattering.
Sudden joy is usually ineffable, but death is rarely inarticulate.

If I had kept a cent for every time I drowned a muskrat in that pond,
I swear to God, he said.
My pinwheel clicked in the wind.
Father lowered me from his shoulders to the red toy wagon.

The morning sex had smoothed our surfaces to a finished glass.
We showered separately.
There among the boiled potatoes resting in a porcelain milk bowl
sank an orange newspaper bag coiled in the shape of an urn.

Fawn-eyed armadillos' foiled plots lay displayed in motor tracks.
Boiled crayfish spread across the wet cement like a deaf man's voice.
Humidity one hundred percent.
New Orleans. My friend bought an alligator head on sale.
I found the gun hidden in thick weeds under an overpass.
Nothing can stop us.

Two Austrian men play chess under a streetlamp
on a board the washed marble of a maple. The metal links
of bicycle chains madly groove to the tick of their own insomnia.
Check, one says, and instantly the other is back in Berchtesgaden.
Two streams converge there, one cataract blue from the Alpine peaks
near the towering Eagle's Nest, the other clear and greenish,
where fish huddle for air. They interlock and form
the teeth of a thresher. Checkmate, says the other.

You know how it feels to inherit tragedy,
sideshow-spawned from the get-go,
crying as you scrub a llama.

In Defense of Escapism as a Means to Express Free Will

Jakob & Wilhelm Grimm tired of enduring the cosmos as *reckless or evil improvisations of deficient angels* & preferred the world of witches' brew & smoke & toads to gunpowder & the negative realities of life. Yet if this were completely true, why have those step-sisters of ill repute slice off their toes to fit a sadomasochistic prince's glass vagina? I'm driving through the Badlands from the Black Hills, SD, mixing metaphors, drinking my coffee black, lonely as the grain is orange. A wall of rushing bison nip at the heels of extinction & I wonder aloud if wondering is what this snake is doing under my car when the repetition of wheels spins the Great Wheel of life & death. The clouds collide to mix a deeper shade of bruise. The snake slithers in the rearview, shrinking to a fine point in my memory, where he'll reside until I imagine him again, in a poem, as Devourer of the World. This near-death experience was his trauma, his Fall. Mankind will pay. On he slithers toward the radiation plant to amass size through physics. There's money to be made in the manufacturing of myth. The Minotaur captured could have made a million for Barnum & Bailey. A minatory bull is nearly redundant if the human element is excluded because the essence is still available & doesn't myth reveal, finally, a certain elimination of the non-derivative Self? We all must press the rock uphill or fuck a swan. It's give in or give up. But what can release us from this illicit sameness? The body raw, gyrating, wanton? What of the mind, inventing the reality it grows into? As the seed imagining its soil, the imagination makes good on its stern stuff:

it improves, it consumes, it relates:

but can it really be *we no longer have command of the data we manipulate*?

Go ask a Grimm.

Go Yankees!

Let's make a bonfire, broil all our hard drives, software, showtunes, codes.
Dear reader,

I tire of the strain you put on witches.

Escapism is the last resort

overlooking the sea with two blinking neon signs: <u>Let's go</u>.

<u>Let's go further</u>.

The Smithsonian Guide to North American Shapes

Wright, Frank Lloyd (1867-1959)

A two-legged horse, propped astride a fence post, yes,
& mark that feeling. Traversing a back road, you spy
its haunches bowing a clutch of barbed wire.

Who would claim the hands that set him there?
For what purpose, what function—simply the geometric?
It's clear we've mishandled the world for long enough.

Men & women have died in urine-damp cells, eyes closed,
mapping out no gardens they can see, alert
as the morning rain shapes sound from rocks when striking—

the human mind must reconstruct the world, in manifold
& then some. But why see everything as X-scape & escape from?
Yes—there is no Unnatural, only standards applied;

what we do with the world is the world doing things to itself.
But that is not to say we should accept a world in full, or the world
within us, or any world that insists on no resistance.

I'd prefer a world, let's say,
that assists us with its clapboard of blue space,
crag terrace & vineland trapeze, structure with scope:

      I'd like to believe in the ground floor's river tongue, chairs
with crystal headaches, concrete planes slashing through
         each narrow path the shocked wind opened to them.

Imagination may one day prove to be the last religion, a space in which
to configure our morality, ore an organic form providing an entertainment
free of responsibility.
         Still, I'd like to think we'd help that horse.

& Such & Such, But Seriously, I Love You I'm Sure I Think Maybe

It was the first night of your hosting
the Oscars, dressed in black and reddening
with the cool diplomacy of my interests.
The floor is grapenuts, several imported cheeses.
One hand with whiskey, the table doused
in chardonnay brought smiles and a clap
from guests this side of devotion, sparing
you nothing as you wiped up with your dress.
In a sparsely lit bar in Santorini, the hugging
desires of waiters slung around your neck,
you proposed the goats had no better job
than sentinels at the stone gates of ancient Thira,
relating how the honeymooning young couple squeezed
out a last minute laugh before the ruins. Let's say
'cocker spaniel' together, quickly, before the sunset
sways, time a'rockin. A'swing. Let's dabble
in a dribble of paint, a pond of watercolors someone
tipped from the vaseline jar where eggs wallowed
like pig's feet. How perfect. I wish we had met when
I was a boy dreaming of being a man dreaming
of cartoon sex in Sunday school. So how's
your crab? your dental plan? I begrudge no one
with an opposing world view. It's like that train
wreck where both conductors saw in advance
the headlines steadily approaching in black
and whitewashed buildings passed like unused
syllables in wake. You sit, adjust your neck with a light
touch and knock the wind out of my proposition.

You hid the rest of the night just of reach,
and if I got too greedy, clenched my fist, I was caught
in what once was called a monkey trap. No net
required, just a hint of bra strap. You said the Self
was a luxury, said people are merely the personification
of others' expectations and fears. Try my batwing soup,
try my father's steel aggression. And after driving hours
along the narrow impassible roadcliffs of the Greek island
we came upon the end of the road where the sea
escaped and in the center of the mountain a door appeared
for which I had no key and for which you were
the riddle and the answer. *How the hell
can you enter that?* Your name is angry beehive
in the teeth of some ur-beast gently rocking
to a tango I'd created while brushing, each sting
a happy horror. That same Halloween night we went home
soaking in a feeling I've felt only once before, watching
the muddied claws of a swallow take flight in a city
even greater in speculative voracity than Florence awash
in bric-a-brack-scattered sunlight off Brunelleschi's dome
but here I'm wrong because that moment was much later.
And then what? Love, that's what. Say something
in your caveman-French. Sexy. Say cocker spaniel.

Listen:Conch

That growing-into thing, motion. How it relies on
everything else around in order to be itself, dragging us about,
as if that-which-it-is, so as to become that-which-it-will-be,
needs no instruction other than resistance.
A wind unwinds the coast of St Augustine, scattering sounds
in a shell I've conjured, shaped with the emery of wishing—
the inward sucking
conch—locating its hollow, which allows for.
Small voices rise faintly beyond the noiseless clapping of sea oats
marshalled on the dunes, at attention. With intention, almost
(and are you even paying attention?)
and it seems, as the tide tumbles toward its reach,
that a god's first voice must have been, if ever it had been,
the simple purity of formless -*ness.*
Each inch a struggle for voice.
See how the spotted whitewash pivots and churns, regroups,
moves again toward the spiral of the conch mired in the breaking waves.
Fills and empties, instruction from the creature
that abandoned it, as we have been abandoned.
I hope you're not paying attention, dear Reed,
when I tell you that life feels mostly like just motion.

For an Autumnal Persona

I think of her as seated in a room
so large she does not notice
she is inside. The ceiling
has stars painted on it
and the boundaries lie well beyond
the earth's curvature.
There are trees dwindling at the fringes.
It is always autumn, even
in summer. There is a mother
and a father somewhere.
There is a sister. An Other.
Sometimes they move like shadows
on the periphery, sometimes
they are close enough so that she knows
they're there, but fails to see them.
She focuses on the invisible forms
of their actions. There is heartbreak,
commitment, resignation, a sense
of scattering. The leaves
are piled up like junk; a place
where roots struggle
to unroot the flowers.
I tell myself that I cannot love someone
who cannot love herself,
but here I am, intrigued, waiting
for the moment she will rise
from the chair and begin to turn, restless,
a mind of unpremeditated words,
a carrier of matters. When she turns
once too often the book falls
from my hands
and I'm forced to start over
in her creation, in my creation,
in whatever drives one
to know another.

Memory of the Body (V)

Memory of a Peninsula Bank on the St Johns,
Falling in Love, Surrounded by Flying Fish

Music happens.
What we call the world is the chance
Collision of notes
On the largest blue instrument I've seen.

But when you speak the strings pucker
& snap.
The drums cave in.
A tuba disappears among the reeds.

***

It has since moved from the immaculate to the material,
changing these notes, this love,
these moments, this interior.

We have each found our separate ends, separately.

I hope you are not lonely when you hear the notes
of this world, sometimes scattered, sometimes frayed,
as if each fin flap contained our making and unmaking.

Because there is still music, in the brush, along the bends
of Turkey Creek, where I was married. Within the hollow
docks of Eau Gallie, the rock jetty of Sebastian Inlet,
the days of rain and how the ocean swifts over the beaches,
the swamps and marshes of the lower basins, and within
the memory of each, and sometimes on the phone, and
sometimes in bad weather.

Godsong

What I first happened to notice
after the Lethe flowed upward—
and I flowed upward with it
into the visible world—
was the dirty, leaf-strewn
mattress under the footbridge
where I guided the fishing rod
through nearby branches. I came up
unexpectedly, where water meets water,
and tied my wood skiff, dropped the oars.
It was the brightest day of the Indian
Summer, and everyone's dreams
were pinched and hung like laundry
from the browning gingko trees.
I could hear the campus students
overhead talking on their way
to classes, discussing subjects
they might possibly forget
in a month's time, though I could forget
nothing—neither their names nor voices;
for in the underworld I was immune.
The river was already beginning
to get mottled with the bodies of the suicides
who wandered too far
into the quotidian, and their imaginations,
through buoyancy of virtue, kept
their corpses afloat in the current
of this river the color of cheap liquor.
I cast out as far as I could
beneath the white pylons
and reeled and reeled, hooking
an elbow, a heel, a tuft of hair;
stacking them up like soldiers on the bank,
my brothers and sisters of forgetting, knowing
I would fish these commingling waters clean,
a menace to no one,
and I would drink and wash, drink and wash
until I could forget the fact that I remain alone
among my fellow sleepers.

On that Brief Happy Sorrow

If we say firmament, yet mean
the crack in space unable
to posit anything but darkness,
then x will still prevail…

by x we mean
that sparse green life grown from soil
settled in the steel bluegray rim
of a bicycle tire raised by a sycamore
that grew through its spokes as a sapling.

by space, the land
that is not land nor air
nor sea.

but is a field but not earth
but contains the firmament:
the unseen that conjures the field
and the earth
and the cracks in the earth
and in each of us.

All day I've been pushing tomato seeds
under the blackred dirt with my thumb
knowing that the morning rain will
draw them upward with a kind of antigravity
and leave them to die bare in the sun.

I continue pushing them down.

It is enough
to imagine that the seeds
take hold of the few deep drops
and make unto themselves, themselves.

Gun Music

Outside the birds rise from chorus
to afterimage.

I wake to investigation—something from the window—
a sound:
a wondrous entering into—
followed by a vision of bleachers' in the fields,
whose arthritic fingers
tear through white cloth to discover
only more white cloth,
the shrouds and chemicals of their own undoing.

Gun music. A hollow branch
broke.
A saturation
that cleans the air of minor distractions.
I listen for the next shot, afraid to touch
the glass. Silence something you can't pick up
to drop.

She will not wake up, has not
heard the discord.

It is startling how the white of her naked back
draped in bedsheets is enough at times.
The blue knots of her spine, arms folded over the white pillows—
the harmony of everyday
glistening with self-assurance.
I would not wake her to the strange truth
that all we own and know
contains the lovely shrapnel of a larger devastation.
Another gunshot, and I grow into it
as its echo wallows,
swells the belly of the city.

I am trapped in the listening.
I am more alive for it.

Theoria Tou Cosmou

The gopher tortoise's shell is a way of reckoning
With the other-than-gopher-tortoise.
The otherworldly rains and sluices along the ravines
Of nose to tail empyrean.

I am. I am not I am. I am not iambs.

I have stolen worlds and words. I am
Rauschenberg late in the Gulf of Mexico evening,
a shard of spring rain shading the sunset
upsetting me at its clarity of composition.
If I were invited into certain drawing rooms
at certain hours, I could be murderous
and resolute. If the evening rain turned
to fog, the shades drawn. But had a businessman
with a plastic pipe forming bubbles—
a pipe not a pipe but a picture—
collapsed at my galoshes—his cardboard hat
falling from his cardboard head—I might have
offered to become him. I'm sure he would have
done the same for me. Whoever I wish to be
has wished me a thousand times over.

Random Form:
     God of Islands.
     …made the firmament, and divided the waters which were under
firmament from the waters which were above firmament.
     God of Water still backpacking the Mariana Trench,
     by which I mean everything is an uncontrollable river.
Random Theory:
     For each impulse a measurable step.
     Let the wanderers charge their science with senses.
     The mind is made to interrupt itself.
     Not changing your mind means your dead.
Random Inclination:
     It's not about what you know.
     It's about what you don't know about what you know.

Memory of the Body (I)
Portage

From wherever you are now
please say something familiar,
something placating as the blood
siphoning behind my fingerprints—
your voice would be worth the death of a thousand cicadas
falling from a tree at once.

Frog cries volley through the smog hovering this marshy reservoir
off the southernmost highway of the county, their questions
baited with resolution, the resignation of the world in them,
a world I recognize by its crockpot scent, its saltwind and swamp cabbage.
Florida.
I have come out here for the romantic pulse
that first anchored my blood
in yours.
If the soupy stain flushed against this unending plain was meant to be dusk it failed
or I did. Transcendence isn't manageable;
Romanticism is hope siphoned through the cipher of a sincere plea for knowledge;
but Nature's pyrotechnics will stall out—
I've drained its batteries a thousand times
trying to urge it to combustion, till the positive spark splits an oak wide open,
spilling out its negative   The Valley of the Shadow of the Heart of Things
and oftentimes I feel emptied with the muck of it.

Indulging the slowmotion momentum of the subaquatic, is how it goes here.
Down the bank, concrete rubblework
dumped by some careless construction crew guides a sluiceway
of frogspawn from a tepid patch of water into the reservoir
and I crouch to watch the shadowing mudbank wring
it brunette roots over this jade&bronze&bone speculum—
this 'compendium of all knowledge':
and If that were true, if this marina of microcosms harbored the *essential*,
the parts containing the whole,
and I as a fervent nonbeliever proclaimed this lowering fog a cloud of unknowing
believing it possible that by reaching the other side, I might find happiness,
or in the least, an understanding of the goodness of love
and all that seeks to fulfill its alter- or bastardiz-ation.

There are smaller things, still. Parts of the parts. Subatomics.
Still-life distilled, a pebbled bottom blossoming into non-being
with a wavelet, announcing yes,
yes, and then obliterated by the gestures of algal grasses, actors
in a fluid rendition of a subway scene:
                        rebounding locomotion: a hell of mercury.

There's this song I sing when I'm lonely and its name is whatever yours was
before you were named.
Please say something familiar, as in
'If you wait half an hour I'll go down with you, let me change into something'
and you changed into so many things.

Cough of the final cirrus clouds of evening, unable
to patch a sudden aneuristic sunset. The landscape paintings
some still hold true, a very real wind across
a very real water. Attempts to manacle a ghost. Verisimilitude itself a crumpled imag
among reeds, blinking its fish scales there
and there—
                a sidewinding missile of logic fractured across an amniotic grid:
'No Truth but in Transit,' Emerson quipped.
So where are we going?
It's like I'm running in circles here.

I opt for simple movement, press my fingers between the sludge-tarred rocks.
Even that feels like running away.
The body resists a world of objects
it seems, in an effort to resist becoming
an object itself.
A body is mostly silence, and water;
so we were mostly something to wade through.
The watery image of my-self fashioned from a single brushstroke is obscured
by the dragonfly
(let it be my testament to a singular place and time)
its wings a staccato prayer upon this mobile heaven
                       —and there the fish glints
(our silences are no longer manageable)
                —and there.

The New Useless

The new poems on Nature
will include a drum of steel, light,
glass, a fuel, garbage that flits around
streetcorners as if the wind
were speaking in tongues. It admits
everything. You probably shouldn't listen
to care. In a book of popular phrases
there will be one about an apple.
Memorize that phrase.
Someday it'll come in handy,
I'm almost sure of it.

Lear on Lear: an Innerview

If you, at the brimming blue of a storm-drawn
          dusk among the black walnuts, sit down
and describe what it is you see
          and what it is you don't see
in the rain growing shorter
          with your fool crying for dicks and toes
who's to call you a liar?
          except that other fool sitting next to you
who with raisins for eyes and teeth
          whittled from fox bone cannot see
but unravels a poke of raw codfish
          asking you what spectral fever
gave him these hands to unwrap with
          and this, my mouth of dried giblets.

Splitting the Lark to Find the Music

A poem of lovers falling in love
and failing at love
cannot be dissected
unless you learn to dissect the lovers;
and lovers cannot learn
to dissect each other
unless they learn to love dissection,
and murder a love by process
of investigation.

Immanence, which is Ever-Transcendence, Slowed

The patient take their waking slowly, slowly
waking
the way a cold moon nagging at the water wakes to its own image
shifting ever silent in what is surface but what is far away
as if desire were a form of inner judgement
like parenthesis in a journal entry.
Desire as a form of discovery beyond analysis,
when the likeliness of a dreamed event transpires
before you can even question it. As in Decorah, mild summer afternoon
when the group of us rented canoes and camped along the silt banks
and woke at dawn surprised that meeting two bald eagles
were two alabaster-colored egrets, strong birds that passed
each other in the wincing sluicelight over trout.
And collided nearly as we fear airplanes tend to;
how part of you wants it to happen, waiting.
And the sudden metal in my mouth, its acrid taste
my body remembered from sampling the possibly medicinal houseplant
whose leaves my cats tend to admire and hack up, the leaves
reticulate as ironworks, willowish strands broadened
to where I image a broadloom wove with woven threads
a florid, fluted airy purple petal. Broad flax inlay bulking at the waxy edge
and darting inward like an arrowhead, which is how humans
in the time of Donne thought of the soul, two lovers staring at each other
from across a semigloss table, the tea pot beginning to murmur,
their eyes fixed to one another's gaze, the twin souls stretched outward
as a form of desire and intertwining in midair above the glass chalice
filled with grapes submerged and rising in water. The transference
of the soul by vision, a way to validate existence. Yes, I see you.
I see you seeing me. I see myself in you, you see? I tie my laces
on the dust-marbled front porch in Iowa autumn, aware of the sexuality
inherent of shoes, the eyelet and the aglet, divorced until their purposes
are exacted by the meaningful existence of the other
as the air has sex with itself in the ash trees overhead and
the colored leaves
glide down over each other
and touch me in this way, in a way I hope I touch them,
as a testament to immanence.

An Encounter

And finally the sunlight tapers across the apartment tops
like the end of a highlighted page, or a postscript
of judgement on an everlasting, perfected industry.
For a few minutes, an eclipse of sighs,
a sense of revelation. I mean the slow-moving traffic
leaking into a knot of itself. I mean the oncoming stars
and plane-sheared clouds that have tricked us from finding heaven there.
It has been like this since blue
jays and twine nests first entered the picture, since I saw my first pigeon
plums for sale on the dirt shoulder
of an unmapable Florida backroad.
The night tumbles into a tail-spin recovery. The sunlight settles
for less than I would have. Amber shellshock almost a color,
everything slightly and subtly disturbed.
So soft not even a beagle with a brass ear
could hear it, the vibrato of living things, this small mending
of day and not-day. The seams show for a brief moment
as the streetlights flicker from *buzz* to *on*.
This is when I feel our lives are constructed of small packets
of misinformation and false leads, cartoonish in the way
good slapstick is. Like prairies of one-legged jugglers
trying to construct a human history in the sky
by tossing up what can never hit the ground lest
it be forgotten. A genuflection of the mind, this smell of earth
and moss basted in a sharp spray of cedar.
Don't you ever just want to eat it all up, all of it?
By false leads I mean what makes me unsure
enough to question the reality of the moment, when faith is the glass
slipper you can almost see yourself in. What can be recovered
from a day? What am I to take into the next red red red fucking dawn,
what am I supposed to lose to make it worth it?
I want the moon to forget itself and the tireless weeping
willow to drop its gold robes right now, and stand naked as a prism,
nascent as an afterthought. And I want someone, any of you,
any of you looking for the heart of the matter along this
our surface selves (can't you feel the dark upon us?)
to stop it, cease, right now! and take me dancing.

Memory of the Body (0)
In Memoriam

big plane

big shadow

Gallery

—pay no attention to that man behind the curtain

Prelude

As cursed to flaw the social fabric at its knots
I claw the seams that bind old hemispheres intact,
release the midnight of your brain, and now construct
as weaponry: your most covert fears, those warlocks,
donning painted masks or floating in a heat-cracked
blown glass sphere, a broiling lava, grayish red,
from which you offer this notorious dispatch:

Carnival.
                        A fenced pit brims with the Barker's cry.
The siamese twins lament for those at the wood
who wake and find they'll never be one traveler—
doppelgänger, seized by luck at the ribs. Scorn-eyed
palmists gather coins behind their bulwark oiled
tent cloths; square-mouthed soothsayers, those apt unravellers
of wallets. Around the caravans, fly-swamped hounds.

I travel indistinctly among these coarse figures.
Coiled on a dusty mattress, the Snake Woman
flashes back her scales, retreats. The florid clowns,
with noses for filthy jokes, invite ten others
and me to sacrifice a stove for their warm van
seating fifty. At Bacchanal parties, a plastic newborn
of my own design is baked in ginger cake. Land

of the macabre, land of ineffable delights—
here is home to shooting galleries, where ducks
are blown through by a pellet and bear hearts, velvet,
dangle loose from chickenwire overhead. Small tykes
dip their paper sticks to pink-dyed maelstroms, or fix
their bites to glossy apples bobbing in a bucket.
Where the Cyclops, banjo-hung, strums some Blue Ridge licks.

On silver floats that could have served a martyr's head,
I, flame's spirit, storm the saxophone-toned port docks;
have with a tugboat's whistle arrived at Bourbon Street.
I am the truth in the cliché.

                                             Festivals led
by large bulls wreathed in flowers lurk the stone Saint Mark's
Piazza in Venice, where the dimming lanterns secrete
a glum aurora, the bulls' brains by broadsword shucked

before the Doge. I, flame's imprint, the voice that pricks,
calling down the thunder of your libido. Think
back to a time when throwing beads could make a shirt shrink
or lifting a skirt could get that cheap date done quick:
who do you suppose? and who wouldn't have? A minx,
your daughter's, pigtails: that parched pig, your son's, dried wick:
No scorn abides me: I don't drive you, but watching, wink.

Test your strength, slap the rust-welted Strongman's scale.
If the Barker hooks your collar with his cane, listen:
> *We didn't lie to you, folks. We told you we had*
> *living, breathing monstrosities. Laugh loud you will,*
> *shudder at them, and yet, but for the accident*
> *of birth, you might live as they've lived...*

Gallery, Where the Memory of the Body (*i*) Converges with its Various Instances

(as it happens   when the music changes,
so does the dance...)

I.

I am that corruptible thing
pruned by incentive   steadily working toward an whole-someness
what doesn't
              kill you   only makes you
                                                  more you
a blue flame at the spirited center
                        But what is it at the periphery
                        that held at this distance
                                desires to be held?

II.

Seated   right-side orchestra   intimate as a belfry sniper to his target, mind-strung to some precarious
logic   I struggle with my placing as the Murray Lewis/Nikolais modern dance troupe attempts to strip the
stage its classical boundaries
in bible belt-buckle Winston Salem, NC
triggering the waterfall of this new millennium

determined to drag the audience down with them:
a caboose of zeros parading into rapids.
Proscenium to midstage   a shooting gallery—
dancers shocked into the aboriginal,
donning glow-in-the-dark masks with eyes   hollowed, barren   brisk
eyes that reveal nothing and mean it.

The gallery
not where you hang   portraits but where
  washed images slide from their celluloid frames
in corners the mind regrets having glanced at, the glances that glance back.

Mascara-purple clowns rush from the wings
and rise like bedsheets snapped and hovering, natural forms
fostered by a thin skein of fabric, sandwiched and sewn
into their costumes. They wear something of the flame.
        And even as it's begun I begin
        to drift
                        outside the theater there's sure to be tires locked in traffic,
            a meter maid registering her day in yawns,
        desolate looks from behind the glass of office buildings,
        bodies stumbling along sidewalks, sidelooks crossing like crossed wires.
            There is no reward in such explicit agony:
I have wished myself dead for lack of meaning. I have stared
the television down till 6am, cramped to fit the sofa,
self-shell humming with the dolor of images. First the image informs,
though when replicated, destroys the first,
until everything is eventual, and empty.

Is there no justifying the habitual?
The television responds by belching data—
JFK's assassination: *back and to the left*,
Discovery Channel's exposé on serial killers: PIGS, flesh masks.
Hitler knuckling his fists in *Triumph des Willens* amid the crowd
       logic. Armed forces destroy the statue of the great Dictator.
          As long as it has a subjective mind fixed to it
     an object can be, and remain, sacred. I'm asking here. As long?
There is the smallest chance
the Apocalypse would come and we'd not
know it, divorced as we can be
from actual events. But not now.
that was just a rumor
the right side of my brain exchanged with the left.

                    (which thinks the other god?

The first wave of the dance waxes supernatural, wanes.
Spirits recall the tilt and lift of feet, of legs
that shook with muscle and cleaved the air
with a windmill's gathered strain.
The dancers' rediscovering of the pressure of stage lights, a new tension in an arena
boxed and climate-controlled. They surge
among wrought-iron jungle gyms like exclamations
or inflections of rhythm, plumbing a new language
or an old one
I've forgotten from birth.

I'm persuaded to enter the funhouse, a labyrinth
constructed to confuse sensibility, mirrors that cripple
the hands like Thalidomide babies'
and staple them to the neck.   *Carnival,*
a reenactment at the Stevens Center.
How easily when watching such dramatics the mind reaches back:
cold-comfort of the Ferris wheel
pinwheels   kielbasas and kraut   apples in their caramel dresses
the electric bloom of cotton candy   bile-leaking children
paraphernalia associated with a good time ad nauseam
dart throw   hay floor   caked shit on the elephant's nozzle
all that jazz.

Always, *there was that time once*, when mortality became real: for some part of me:
          hair spread out behind the neck like some encumbered ideogram,
               flush against the painted plywood, the blinded woman waited
                    to bow until the final lemon-slice of Bowie knife
                         had wedged its steely truth between her thighs.

                    Once, I imagine remembering, I watched the carnies set up tent.
                              A nocturnal, traveling nation,
                    Tired faces squinteyed in the palatable dust, hands up
                    shielding smoke drafts loosened from a mobile kitchen.
                    Eight-buck hourly workers come from whatever town
                         to work switchboards, watching the children's rides
                              Circulate like a spun coin dying down.
(A sneeze brings me back, but there I go again   here I go   somewhere I go somewhere
safer   **III.**

It is a bit odd, the first time you remember the future. Framed in iron crossbeams like someone you know waving from a distance, but green as an oil slick, this woman—the F Train jostling toward the city from Brooklyn. It has been ten years since I wrote this poem. Christo and Jeanne-Claude have shuttled the world under a trellis of saffron in the park. Last week three young boys shot a playwright in the subway, but today it is cold and bright, buttons snapping under scarves. Johnny's book with the comedian is done and I have Chris's pages on new American religious movements tucked in my back pocket—old wine in new bottles   but in ten years rushing backward from those gates I will begin this, revising and truncating, only to look upon it now as someone else's handiwork. A line here and there slipped from the ether like a slideshow. The way it stales. My revision is working toward a lesser vision. It is saddening,
a little, not to trust the art of cleverly developed taglines of the poetry of the future
the brandable, incapable *pop buzz snap you*   a loss of *image sizzle conflict us* that still drives a bulk of our narratives. There were those moments in that auditorium watching the dance that produced a very different happening within me as I watched: a parallel, a progress, a slim offering of comparable compatibles)

II. The midnight interlude of things that go chitty chitty bang
bang in the dark, light-retardant, sheathed in unitards of coalblack lycra,
the dancers collapse desire: (it is neither wanting or wanting to not want):
Dr. Seuss characters, worm-necked, crazy with appendages,
they body-chant a sluice of calculations,
choreography that has us creaking in our seats.
Great French curves and ruthless angles and lighting effects,
bodies trolling in porpoise locomotion. Rise, arch
and grip again. Master me, momentum. A work,
a wrench, a word thrown
into the bodyworks.

The dance is filmic because of its networking roots—
Every film a documentary of itself
and the way it was made, said Wenders, as if
the world were finally fiction,
forcing spectators to grope about the freedom
of a character's naiveté, a character that is innately them, in their seats, struggling with a new place, a new time.
We are a cinema of sorts, almost in the way of Sisyphus,
an undesirable amount of climaxes,
chased down again, and again,
the extraordinary voyage to some peak.

Carousing, maneuvering, lollygagging, the body's banner
for a ritual of coercion, the dancers bring the news of the terrible
Us, approaching rapidly and from all sides. Figures streamlined across the stage, rotating,
bomb-diving from their awkward perches. A sweat droplet lineates a course
down and over the folded topography of my stomach
                              (I'm thinking Maya Lin [touch me] and the waters [sweat of man]).
Bittersweet, collecting each of us by our paper wings,
the music unites and divides us, each attuned to different ranges,
invites us in, takes our coats
and sends us to the cellar or the attic of our dreams.
How the music shifts so sudden and slight:
carousel symphonies, magical in their discourses,
pitch your past to you like a roustabout, droning, droning,
until it drops,
livid as the music of a Texas Instrument.

I await the vanishing hour, when
we again become the audience
of our own lives,
a forest of tiered faces, roaming sidewalks,
rotating like unbound personals in a public dryer.

Nikolais understood our obsession with carnality,
knew Poe's imp, knew das Es, knew the pimp in us.
It's hard to shake that there's something controlling
each lift and plunge—   some universal,   some way of being
stripped of self-realization, which keeps it from tragedy.

Can we claim this?

Some have said the difference between the beautiful and the sublime
is that the sublime could kill us but chooses not to.
That means the sublime has choice.
That means beauty kills us.
I think the difference between the two is that I get to decide which kills
me more
beautifully.   Did someone just sing *duende*?

We will assimilate whatever comes our way: or give it a good honest shot:
We would eat the earth whole if we get it down our throats:
Americana
The world will never yield *enough*—
small iced blisters of road oil,
sheepskin bucketseats.

I'm zoning.
Behind the ten spirits now on stage, two oversized and arresting bullseyes.

Hunchbacked and sickle-celled,
    myopic as gods, flippant, hosts to all things
        microscopic, beautiful as verdicts, the clowns onstage—rather *the headless torsos*
           thereof—prance around unheard like shouts from another world.
             This dance, like me, tore up through the turf of the 70's.

                It didn't take me long to see beyond improbability.
                 One summer, I jumped off an 80' bridge with a
                    Navy Seal who did a front flip, dipped
                      the cold blue clean as a fountain pen.
                 I jumped next and, for less than four seconds,
                      rode my first and last manatee.

Stonewalling.
Writhing in their protective shadows, mix&matched like combines,
the dancers flare out their entrails.
Not grotesque, not carrion, not the damp cinder-smell of lotion
sizzling on a mother's napalmed arm, outstretched; rather,
by way of deformity, an intuition of the self
seen the way the surgeon sees.
        The dead have always been responsible
        for the doctor's knowledge.
And I feel better for it.

The past returns like a swift kick—
these bare thought brackish in the black-water dusk of burnt&creamless coffee, a midnight
twelve-hour nicotine drive to Florida, the sinus-headaches
of inspiration and guises of unity that guide me through morality.
That boy in summer trunks, whose fingers I have outgrown,
laughing wildly, combing his hair back in a mirror, sure as shit
he's gonna die before he reaches the age of me.

Yet the dancers persevere (this does not concern them), sweating
and counting steps, locating blocking, so that the audience
might witness the whole while they adopt the parts.
Yet the whole was never theirs to give.
It rests in my making and imagination.

Males optimum because they are fewer in number.
The female dancer must fight for positioning.
She's always down, blue as an article, always
warring in the trenches and sentenced to live by body-wit
and secondhand nature; and until the dance-world's the better,
as if not male meant merely noun, she'll be
genderless in English,
thing'd to death.

III. [An Intermission in the Form of a
Love Poem Written 10 Years Before]

3 Meditations On a Woman

She works in the moments that break down.
The bone, the gut, the delicate pads of feet that bubble
under weight,
it's all movement. Air with its medicinal tendencies
strives to keep the dancers off their feet.
When we talk of bodies colliding we reach somewhere
beyond
the constellations, somewhere beyond inevitability
and get our hands dirty with the muck and grime of
chance, where patterns leap beyond the billionth digit
and land

       (just before the stage spreads its wings)

softly
and kick
and disappear into the wings.

   ***

The fruit hangs not upside down from the branch
    but rises toward earth, balancing between
    a rootless sun and soil. The woman drifts
    between the fruit's lack of self-awareness
    & the ghost who lives in its own memory.
This is the Sante Fe of our existence, mountains on
all sides, the adobes having sidled each
    other for decades, slowly evolving into

familiarity. Small animals slide their bellies across
        the hot sand, searching for shade. Daylight
        huddles over the crouching red rock of
        eastern mountains, where the cacti are
        simply scrub brush with a college education.
Sit down & have a drink. Even the sun is
outshined
        by this tequila. If we stand up again, we
        hang from our shoes. But if we jump, we are
lost somewhere between.

***

Woman,
mythic creature of vapor, piecemeal of old lovers
conjured up from
a hawk's beak, mouse's paw, eye of newt, scales of a
tongueless dragon;
more than a sum of parts,
the very thing I feared, the woman born holy
without a scripture to attest
(let this be your gospel)
the inertly savage, composed of raw fire and bled
horizons.
Quick to dissolve in the shimmer-shine of quartz
traveling through the jagged soul of rock
bursting out as a spectrum across our bedroom wall.

This is how love is, the shadowy underbelly
of the leaf wet with morning
forced up and out over the sidewalks by a breeze
exposed
spun across a shallow pool that reflects its other half
or stirs to mud.

II. Sports coat. black on white with black
bowties, Led Zeppelin tshirts, berets, stuffy aromatic patchouli,
sequined gowns, cardigans, blue-haired young and old:
the genetic makeup of the audience.
We're the spectacle. We've been practicing all our lives.

Courting disaster
my brother, Jason, and I went to a party
at an abandoned (but not) condemned (hardly) Spanish/
stucco two-story tenement infested with teen-age drug dealers,
squatters, bikers, a Vietnam vet telling us how he crouched behind boulders,
shooting without aim. A drug-dealer pistol-whipped
a biker that night. Later on, with Orion hunting the Bear,
I pushed Jason forward into a cavern
of junked cars as the bullets whipped by us like promises
neither of us wanted to accept.

Later, while cruising down US-1,
a buddy of mine
tacked a 45mph red stiletto into
a whore's head with a lead
fishing weight,

a pyramid-pronged sinker.
Sometimes the real is too strong
to witness and believe and pass on,
or write, or re-believe and confront.
It grows muscles and tongues, gets mean and drunk.
Better to circle the thing with abstractions than
pin it down, where it can stare back at you.
But what is Truth without Experience, and Experience without Record?

I heard a comedian say that when he died
he would donate his body to science
fiction: lungs of an epoch, heart of bloodless revolutions,
the intestine-wrap of history, spine of hope,
brain of utopias, something man makes unto himself.
If all this could be had with one person,
who wouldn't murder?

Back in the doghouse, looking
to do a little damage control for his life, my dad
made his way to lockdown in the jail's lockup.
There he preached the Word
to inmates who pissed themselves, made shanks from spoons,
soap guns, lead paintballs from the unraveling walls. One guy
set his bed afire and searched for sleep.
Father. All this while busy packing up from a wife and three sons.
At some point these truths surface as mere facts to me.

The dance doesn't push you away from it,
it simply defines the line between you and it
like an Escher pen&ink,
then crumples the page.
IV. Who isn't becoming his or her own eleventh dimension? Ever smallering. **II.**
At nine and ten, the head lice took up camp
and had to be dragged out with a metal-toothed comb.
Eleven, before the doctor could say it, I diagnosed
myself with scabies. Lord knows how.
By twelve I was having sex between the layers of a folded foldout couch.

A woman sits next to me with two gold crosses,
braided and faith-plated, slung from her collarbones,
one inoculating the other   (how long have I not been watching?)—
How does one's subjectivity locate that angle
of protraction, reach out at a slant, and finally
take hold of things, of objects, which invites our speculation?
We come into this world
and leave as objects. Can I not sense myself
pining though a wilderness of me,
an objective thing, restless, primitive, coping?

Double-music, karaoke style, syncopation.
Sometimes the prelude,
lifted through the rafters
by an original score,
flatlines for a duration and then dives straight down into the epilogue
and lives.

This is what I mean by liberty,
something that finds purpose not by its ends,
but by the arc of movement
somewhere between the struggle of being
and being raw material.

Wanting to reach the *closeness*,
that ever-life quality until you die,
and remain an Impermanent
among impermanent Others
that nestle up with their cold feet,
coffee-breath at 8am, face and legs swollen from sweat-salt and sleep.
Can I say with a clear conscience
I am no *thing*
when I feel like mere landscape at times: in the Gassian sense:
I am that nervous tension and resolve,
the ghostly referent of a pronoun:
Snow sometimes affects me as much as my neighbor's voice.
Thing-ness, my buddy calls it, affirming
life by hating death, detesting it,
(isn't it natural to detest the experience of Nature?)
to be independent yet unified by situation
with things like dented fenders and glabellar creases,
dogs, orgasms, snow cones, AIDS,
women that cry on your shirt at the Post Office.

I wish there had been a gull named Communal With Situation,
A shrub named Now & Until the End.
I would have used them in so many poems.

The past is that heat of your palm,
pressed against a child's forehead,
whispering "I feel nothing wrong,"
sheathing her in comforters, checking
under the bed, in the closet, reassuring her.
Then, plugging in the night-light
shaped as a cartoon figure, smiling,
the light elongating
across the almond wall and thumbtacked posters.
Some of us shut her door.
Some of us invite her into our beds.
But at some point, we all sleep.

I'm sure now there is no outside.

Some rubber light, fetal-dream.
A man kicked in the street looks this way,
how I crouch in my seat.

The music shifts, angling for tension.
The implosion of funhouse-techno-rave catches the auditorium
at its throat. The dancers rise, facing out,
their lightbulb heads rock back and forth behind the waist-high backdrop.
The audience has shifted.
Music fuzzes, blurs everything to nuance, twilling,
followed by the pump-speed rifle fire issued from the loudspeakers.

The masks rock back and forth.
And when they surface, smiles blown to smithereens by an audience
that evades us and whose bodies we wear,
large portions of the dancer's masks rise up missing, a media event,
stamped with large shards of black tape as if that part were shot off,
slapped back with a wallop,
and they rock, free now from foreheads
and cheeks and noses, like characters in fiction,
until they rock invisible, and drop.

White lights, the stage liquefied.
They stand and bow, smiling,
maskless, their costumes gripping their insulated bodies.
And of course, we all rise to our feet.
We had been on our knees since the beginning.

Joe Pan is the author of two poetry collections, *Autobiomythography & Gallery* (BAP) and *Hiccups* (Augury Books). He is the publisher and managing editor of Brooklyn Arts Press, serves as the poetry editor for the arts magazine *Hyperallergic*, and is the founder of the services-oriented activist group Brooklyn Artists Helping. His piece "Ode to the MQ-9 Reaper," a hybrid work about drones, was excerpted and praised in *The New York Times*. In 2015 Joe participated in Lower Manhattan Cultural Council's Process Space artist residency program on Governors Island. Joe attended the Iowa Writers' Workshop, grew up along the Space Coast of Florida, and now lives in Williamsburg, Brooklyn.

Visit him at JoePan.com.

Made in the USA
Monee, IL
07 July 2026

56551170R00062